jams AND preserves

jams AND preserves

gina steer

Love Food™ is an imprint of Parragon Books Ltd

Parragon
Queen Street House
4 Queen Street
Bath BA1 1HE

ISBN: 978-1-4075-0366-0

Printed in China

Photography: Clive Bozzard-Hill
Home economists: Valerie Barrett and Sandra Baddeley

Produced by the Bridgewater Book Company Ltd

Notes for the Reader
This book uses both metric and imperial measurements. Follow the same units of measurement throughout; do not mix metric and imperial. All spoon measurements are level: teaspoons are assumed to be 5 ml, and tablespoons are assumed to be 15 ml. Unless otherwise stated, milk is assumed to be full fat, eggs and individual vegetables such as potatoes are medium and pepper is freshly ground black pepper. Recipes using raw or very lightly cooked eggs should be avoided by infants, the elderly, pregnant women, convalescents and anyone suffering from an illness. The times given are an approximate guide only.

contents

introduction

What could be more satisfying than having a row of home-made preserves in your cupboard?

Whether it is a jam, chutney, pickle, relish or conserve, there really is nothing better. Why? You may

ask. Well, it is simple. Making your own preserves ensures that you have total control over the quality

of the ingredients used, as well as ensuring that there are no hidden extras, such as artificial colours

or flavourings. Plus, of course, if you grow your own fruit or vegetables, it is a great way to use your

own produce, especially when you find you have a glut of a particular food. Preserves also make an

excellent gift and one that everyone would be proud to give and more than happy to receive.

Equipment

It is not strictly necessary to buy special equipment for making preserves, but if you plan to make a few there are several pieces that make life just that little bit easier.

Preserving pan – The first piece you need is a preserving pan. This needs to be heavy and made of aluminium, stainless steel or copper. Look for a wide diameter pan, which allows for maximum evaporation when boiling to setting point. Most preserving pans have a large handle that goes from one side to the other for ease of handling. They normally have sloping sides, which help to maintain a full rolling boil. A non-reactive interior, such as enamel, aluminium, stainless steel or non-stick, is best when making chutney or pickles. This will ensure the acidic content does not react with the pan. When using the pan for jams, jellies or conserves you need to make sure that it is large enough. It needs to be no more than half full after the sugar has dissolved, otherwise the contents will boil over when you are boiling to setting point. Very large saucepans can be used providing they are about 5.7 litres/10 pints in capacity. These will have a lid, which is useful when cooking fruits and vegetables that need a long simmering time. The preserve will take longer to reach setting point in a saucepan because the surface area is not as large.

Long-handled wooden spoon – An essential piece of equipment that enables the successful stirring of fruits or vegetables without the spoon falling into the hot liquid. Look for wooden spoons that are at least 30 cm/12 inches, better still those that are 38 cm/15 inches.

Long-handled slotted spoon – These are ideal for skimming off any stones or scum that floats to the top when boiling to setting point.

Jam/sugar thermometer – When making jams, jelly or conserves the hot liquid needs to be brought to setting point. You can try the saucer method (see page 10) but the thermometer is more accurate.

Jelly bag and stand – This is for straining off the juices from the fruits that have been simmered slowly to extract all the liquid possible. The juice is then boiled with sugar to make the jelly. You can improvise by suspending a jelly bag from the legs of an upturned chair or stool. The stand, which it is possible to buy, is attached to the sides of a large bowl. It is essential that the jelly bag is scalded with boiling water before using and the contents should be left in a draught-free place and not squeezed, to allow all the juice to drip through. This will ensure a cloud-free jelly. Wash thoroughly after use and scald each time. The bowl should also be scalded before use.

Funnel – This has a wide neck and sits comfortably in the neck of a jam jar, allowing the jars to be filled with minimal spillage.

Slicer – This can be either an attachment to a free-standing mixer or a tabletop slicer. Many food processors also have a slicing attachment. This is useful for making marmalade. The peel of Seville oranges is far tougher than other citrus fruits and it needs to be finely shredded to make it palatable. Some recipes soak the shredded peel for a long period or simmer for 30 minutes covered with water before using in the preserve. The peel can be cut into fine shreds with a sharp kitchen knife, but using a slicer is easier.

Cherry stoner – Useful when making preserves with fresh cherries, this will help to prevent your hands from being stained by the juice.

Sieve – If you need to use a sieve, ensure that it is nylon to avoid any tainting of the food. Metal could discolour the fruits.

Jars – Clean jars are an essential part of preserving. It is a good idea to save the jars from commercial products. Make sure the jars are scrupulously clean and sterilized before use. When required, wash well in plenty of hot soapy water, rinse thoroughly in very hot water to remove all traces of soap and dry off. Place upturned jars on a baking sheet in a warm oven at 140°C/275°F/Gas Mark 1 for 15 minutes to sterilize them, then place the sterilized jars upside down on a clean tea towel until required. Allow the preserve, once setting point has been reached, to stand for 10–15 minutes before potting. Fill the jars while they are still warm. Any glass jars can be used as long as they are warm and sterilized.

Muslin – This is ideal for making small bags to enclose pips, spices or other ingredients that need removing after boiling. Cut out a square: the size will be governed by the amount to be tied up. Place the ingredients in the centre and fold up into a pouch. Tie with a long piece of string and attach to one of the preserving pan handles and ensure that the bag is immersed in the liquid. It is then easy to remove at the end of cooking.

Covers – Once made, the preserves should be covered immediately with a waxed disc and left until cold. Once completely cold, cover with cellophane covers, which are lightly dampened and secured with an elastic band. Alternatively, use tight-fitting, screw-top lids. Don't use metallic lids when making pickles and chutneys. Label and date clearly then store in cool, dark cupboards.

Testing for a set

The easiest way to test is with a jam/sugar thermometer, where the preserve needs to reach 105°C/220°F. Place the thermometer in the pan when boiling rapidly, until the mercury reaches the correct temperature. Alternatively, try the saucer test. Place a few saucers in the refrigerator when the preserve starts to boil, then when it has been boiling rapidly for the stated time, place a small teaspoonful of the mixture on a cold saucer and leave for a couple of minutes. Take the pan off the heat when testing for a set. If the jam on the saucer wrinkles when a clean finger is pushed across the surface of it, then setting point has been reached. If it is not ready, return to a rolling boil and retest in a few minutes. Take care not to overboil.

Ingredients

The condition of the produce used is extremely important when making preserves. The fruit needs to be ripe but still firm, without any rotten or bad pieces. Vegetables also need to be free from bruises or damaged pieces. Both fruit and vegetables need to be very fresh but it is possible to freeze them for later use. This is very useful when making marmalade; Seville oranges are seasonal and only appear in the shops around the end of January. Buy and freeze immediately, then thaw and use within 6 months. When using for marmalade, use a little extra than the recipe to allow for any loss of pectin while frozen.

Setting agents – Jams, jellies, marmalades and conserves will only set if they have the correct amount of setting agent and sugar. The setting agent is pectin – either natural or commercial. Commercial pectin is made from apples and is in liquid form. It is generally added after boiling and is normally used for fruits that have a low natural pectin level. It is also used for preserves where the fruit is only lightly boiled so as to retain larger pieces of fruit. Fruits with a high pectin content include blackcurrants, Bramley apples, crab-apples, cranberries, damsons, gooseberries, lemons, limes, Seville oranges, quinces and redcurrants. Fruits with a medium pectin content include dessert apples, apricots, blueberries, blackberries, greengages, loganberries, plums and raspberries. Fruits with a low pectin content include bananas, carrots, cherries, figs, grapes, marrows, melons, peaches, nectarines, pineapple, rhubarb and strawberries.

Sugar – In the UK we have preserving sugar and jam sugar that have been specifically produced for preserves. Preserving sugar should be used with fruits that have a high pectin content. The large sugar crystals allow the water to move freely between the crystals on the base of the pan, which will reduce burning and create less froth and scum during boiling. Jam sugar has a balanced amount of natural pectin and citric acid, which helps fruits with a low pectin content to set. If it just says 'sugar' in a recipe, then use granulated sugar. Often this will mean that the recipe will be using pectin as well.

Lemon and lime juice – These contain a high pectin level and can be added to the pan with the fruit to help with the set. Citric acid can also be used. It is important that the correct amount of pectin acid and sugar are used, as both are imperative to obtain a good set.

Vinegar – This is a preserving agent and is the most important part of any pickle or chutney. Use the best quality, as this will have a high acetic quality. Distilled or white vinegar is best used for preserves where a lighter colour is required. Malt vinegar gives a darker colour as well as a slightly better flavour. Most pickles and chutneys improve with keeping for at least two weeks to allow the flavours to mature. Infusing with spices can also enhance both vinegars.

Salt – Table or cooking salt is used to make a brine solution to soak vegetables or some fruits that are going to be used in pickles. Ensure that the foods soaked in brine are thoroughly rinsed before use.

Jams and conserves are a mixture of fruits and sugar which are boiled together to produce a delicious spread that can be used on breads, scones, tarts, cakes and desserts. The high content of sugar preserves the fruit and helps to prevent the growth of bacteria. This is why reduced-sugar jams should be kept in the refrigerator once opened and used quickly. Jams with a higher sugar content will keep in a cool cupboard for two to three months if the lids are screwed down tightly.

jams and conserves

Other flavours can be added, if liked, to the recipes in this chapter. Spices to try are lightly bruised lemongrass stalks, star anise, cardamom or vanilla pods. Tie in a small piece of muslin and discard after boiling.

Classic strawberry jam

MAKES about 450 g/1 lb

1.5 kg/3 lb 5 oz ripe, unblemished whole strawberries, hulled and rinsed

2 freshly squeezed lemons, juice sieved

1.5 kg/3 lb 5 oz jam sugar

1 tsp butter

Place the strawberries in a preserving pan with the lemon juice, then simmer over a gentle heat for 15–20 minutes, stirring occasionally, until the fruit has collapsed and is very soft.

Add the sugar and heat, stirring occasionally, until the sugar has completely dissolved. Add the butter, then bring to the boil and boil rapidly for 10–20 minutes, or until the setting point is reached.

Leave to cool for 8–10 minutes, skim then pot into warmed sterilized jars and cover the tops with waxed discs. When completely cold, cover with cellophane or lids, label and store in a cool place.

Cook's tip: Other flavours can be added if liked. Add 2 lightly bruised lemongrass stalks and 4 lightly bruised green cardamom pods. Discard the spices before potting.

Spicy blueberry jam

MAKES about 1.5 kg/3 lb 5 oz

675 g/1 lb 8 oz blueberries, rinsed

225 ml/8 fl oz freshly squeezed orange juice

2 whole star anise

1 cinnamon stick, lightly bruised

500 g/1 lb 2 oz granulated sugar

175 ml/6 fl oz liquid pectin

Place the blueberries in a preserving pan with the orange juice. Tie the spices up in a small piece of muslin and add to the pan, then simmer over a gentle heat for 20 minutes, or until very soft.

Add the sugar and cook gently, stirring occasionally, until the sugar has completely dissolved. Bring to the boil and boil for 3 minutes, then remove from the heat and stir in the pectin. Leave to cool slightly.

Discard the spices then pot into warmed sterilized jars and cover the tops with waxed discs. When completely cold, cover with cellophane or lids, label and store in a cool place.

Cook's tip: Try using a vanilla pod, split open, in place of the cinnamon and star anise.

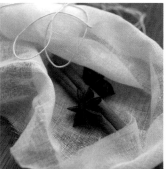

Cherry with brandy jam

Roughly chop the cherries and place in a large preserving pan with the lemon juice. If using citric or tartaric acid, add to the pan with the water. Place the pan over a gentle heat, cover and simmer gently for 20 minutes, or until the cherries have collapsed and are very soft.

Add the sugar and heat, stirring frequently, until the sugar has completely dissolved. Add the butter and brandy, bring to the boil and boil rapidly for 3 minutes. Remove from the heat and stir in the pectin.

Leave to cool for 10 minutes then pot into warmed sterilized jars and cover the tops with waxed discs. When completely cold, cover with cellophane or lids, label and store in a cool place.

Cook's tip: Other spirits or liqueurs can be used in place of the brandy. Try Kirsch, Cointreau or a whisky liqueur.

MAKES about 2.25 kg / 5 lb

1.8 kg/4 lb dark cherries, such as Morello, rinsed and stoned

125 ml/4 fl oz freshly squeezed lemon juice or 1 1/2 tsp citric or tartaric acid

150 ml/5 fl oz water (optional)

1.25 kg/2 lb 12 oz granulated sugar

1 tsp butter

4 tbsp brandy

225 ml/8 fl oz liquid pectin

Plum jam

MAKES about 2.25 kg / 5 lb

1.5 kg/3 lb 5 oz ripe but firm plums, rinsed

450 ml/16 fl oz water

1.5 kg/3 lb 5 oz preserving sugar

1 tsp butter

Discard any damaged plums, then cut in half and remove the stones. Crack a few of the stones open and remove the kernels and reserve.

Place the plums, reserved kernels and water in a preserving pan, bring to the boil then reduce the heat and simmer for 40 minutes, or until soft and pulpy. Add the sugar and heat gently, stirring frequently, until the sugar has completely dissolved, then add the butter. Bring to the boil and boil rapidly for 10–15 minutes, or until the setting point is reached.

Leave to cool for 8 minutes then pot into warmed sterilized jars and cover the tops with waxed discs. When completely cold, cover with cellophane or lids, label and store in a cool place.

Cook's tip: Add some spices to give a distinctive flavour, such as 6 lightly cracked cardamom pods or 2–3 lightly bruised lemongrass stalks.

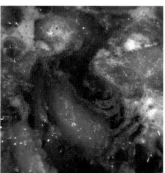

Peach and passion fruit jam

MAKES about 2.5 kg / 5 lb 8 oz

900 g/2 lb ripe, firm peaches, rinsed

4 ripe passion fruits

150 ml/5 fl oz freshly squeezed lemon juice

900 g/2 lb preserving sugar

Make a small cross at the stalk end of each peach and place in a large bowl. Cover with boiling water and leave to stand for 2–3 minutes. Drain and leave to cool. When cool enough to handle, peel off the skins. Cut the peaches in half and discard the stones. Place the fruit in a preserving pan. Cut the passion fruit in half, scoop out the pulp and seeds and add to the peaches.

Add the lemon juice and sugar, place over a gentle heat and simmer for 30 minutes, or until the fruit is soft and pulpy. Bring to the boil and boil rapidly for 15 minutes, or until the setting point is reached.

Leave to cool for 10–15 minutes before potting into warmed sterilized jars and cover the tops with waxed discs. When completely cold, cover with cellophane or lids, label and store in a cool place.

Cook's tip: Passion fruit are ripe and ready to use when very wrinkled.

Quick apricot jam

Place the apricots in a microwaveable bowl, add the lemon juice and water, cover and cook on high for 5–6 minutes, or until very soft. Remove and pour into a preserving pan. Alternatively, cook the apricots with the lemon juice in a heavy based saucepan for 20–25 minutes until soft. Remove and pour into a preserving pan.

Add the sugar and cook gently, stirring occasionally, until the sugar has completely dissolved. Stir in the cranberries, bring to the boil and boil for 15 minutes, or until the setting point is reached. Remove from the heat and leave to stand for 5 minutes. Stir in the flaked almonds.

Pot into warmed sterilized jars and cover the tops with waxed discs. When completely cold, cover with cellophane or lids, label and store in a cool place.

Cook's tip: The kernels from the stones can be added if liked. Crack open a few stones, remove the kernels and blanch before adding to the pan with the fruit.

MAKES about 2.7 kg/6 lb

1.8 kg/4 lb ripe apricots, rinsed and chopped, stones discarded

150 ml/5 fl oz freshly squeezed lemon juice

225 ml/8 fl oz water

1.8 kg/4 lb jam sugar

55 g/2 oz dried cranberries

25 g/1 oz flaked almonds

Melon and ginger jam

MAKES about 900 g/2 lb

1 Galia melon, about 450 g/1 lb
(peeled weight)

1 large wedge watermelon, about
450 g/1 lb (peeled weight)

900 g/2 lb granulated sugar

85 ml/3 fl oz lemon juice

7.5-cm/3-inch piece fresh root
ginger, peeled and grated

125 ml/4 fl oz liquid pectin

Peel the melons, discarding the seeds, and finely chop the flesh. Place in a large bowl and sprinkle
with 450 g/1 lb of sugar and the lemon juice. Cover and leave overnight.

The next day, place the melon with the liquid that has been extracted overnight into a preserving
pan, together with the grated ginger, and simmer over a gentle heat for 30 minutes, or until very
soft. Add the remaining sugar and heat, stirring occasionally, until the sugar has completely
dissolved. Bring to the boil and boil rapidly for 3 minutes. Remove the pan from the heat and stir
in the pectin.

Leave to cool for 10 minutes then pot into warmed sterilized jars and cover the tops with waxed
discs. When completely cold, cover with cellophane or lids, label and store in a cool place.

Cook's tip: Add some chopped stem ginger to the pan with the pectin.

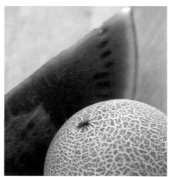

Pineapple and mint jelly

MAKES about 1 kg/2 lb 4 oz

1 large ripe pineapple, about
800 g/1 lb 12 oz (peeled weight)

2 Bramley apples, about 450 g/
1 lb (total weight)

1.2 litres/2 pints water

few fresh mint sprigs

about 675 g/1 lb 8 oz preserving
sugar (see method)

2 tbsp chopped fresh mint

green food colouring (optional)

Peel the pineapple and cut lengthways into 4 wedges. Chop the pineapple, including the core, into small chunks and place in a preserving pan. Chop the apples (do not peel or core) and add to the pan with the water and mint sprigs. Bring to the boil then reduce the heat and simmer for 1 hour, or until the fruits are very soft. Leave to cool slightly before straining through a jelly bag.

Once all the juice has been extracted, measure and return to the rinsed-out preserving pan. Add the sugar, allowing 450 g/1 lb of sugar for every 600 ml/1 pint of juice. Heat gently, stirring frequently, until the sugar has completely dissolved. Bring to the boil and boil rapidly for 10–15 minutes, or until the setting point is reached.

Remove and leave to cool for at least 5 minutes. Skim, if necessary, then stir in the chopped mint and green food colouring (if using). Pot into warmed sterilized jars and cover the tops with waxed discs. When completely cold, cover with cellophane or lids, label and store in a cool place.

Cook's tip: Replace the mint with a few sprigs of fresh rosemary or basil. This is perfect for serving with meat dishes.

P
a

A
fr
10

w

C
af

Pepper and chilli jelly

MAKES about 675 g/1 lb 8 oz

3–5 serrano red chillies,
or according to taste

8 red peppers, deseeded and
roughly chopped

2 Bramley apples, washed and
roughly chopped

150 ml/5 fl oz white wine vinegar

1.4 litres/2½ pints water

1 tbsp coriander seeds,
lightly crushed

5-cm/2-inch piece fresh root
ginger, peeled and grated

about 900 g/2 lb preserving sugar
(see method)

225 ml/8 fl oz liquid pectin

Cut 2–3 chillies in half, discard the seeds and chop the flesh. Place the chillies, peppers and apples in a preserving pan with the vinegar, water, coriander seeds and ginger. Bring to the boil, then reduce the heat and simmer for 1 hour, or until the peppers are very tender. Strain through a jelly bag.

Once all the liquid has been extracted, measure and return to the rinsed-out preserving pan. Add the sugar, allowing 450 g/1 lb of sugar for every 600 ml/1 pint of pepper juice. Discard the seeds from 1–2 of the remaining chillies and reserve. (The other chilli could be used if a very hot jelly is preferred.) Heat gently, stirring frequently, until the sugar has completely dissolved, then bring to the boil and boil rapidly for 3 minutes, or until the setting point is reached.

Leave to cool for 5 minutes. Skim, then stir in the pectin and the reserved chopped chillies. Pot into warmed sterilized jars and cover the tops with waxed discs. When completely cold, cover with cellophane or lids, label and store in a cool place.

Cook's tip: Take care when handling chillies: avoid touching your eyes or any other sensitive parts of the body until the hands have been thoroughly washed.

Wine jelly

MAKES about 675 g/1 lb 8 oz

450 g/1 lb Bramley apples, washed and cut into chunks

600 ml/1 pint water

1 bottle red wine, such as claret

about 675 g/1 lb 8 oz preserving sugar (see method)

Place the apples in a preserving pan together with the water and wine. Bring to the boil, then reduce the heat and simmer for 30 minutes, or until the apples are very soft and pulpy. Strain through a jelly bag.

Once all the juice has been extracted, measure and return to the rinsed-out preserving pan. Add the sugar, allowing 450 g/1 lb of sugar for every 600 ml/1 pint of juice. Heat gently, stirring frequently, until the sugar has completely dissolved. Bring to the boil and boil rapidly for 15 minutes, or until the setting point is reached.

Leave to cool slightly, skim, then pot into warmed sterilized jars and cover the tops with waxed discs. When completely cold, cover with cellophane or lids, label and store in a cool place.

Cook's tip: Other wines, such as white or rosé, can be used as well.

Tomato jelly

Place the 900 g/2 lb tomatoes in a preserving pan. Chop the orange and add to the pan. Lightly bruise the lemongrass and add to the pan with the ginger, star anise, whole cloves, water and vinegar.   Place over a gentle heat, cover and simmer for 40–50 minutes, or until the tomatoes are very soft and pulpy. Leave to cool slightly before straining through a jelly bag.

Once all the juice has been extracted, measure and return to the rinsed-out preserving pan. Add the sugar, allowing 450 g/1 lb of sugar for every 600 ml/1 pint of juice. Heat gently, stirring frequently, until the sugar has completely dissolved, then stir in the tomato purée. Bring to the boil and boil rapidly for 10–20 minutes, or until the setting point is reached.

Leave to cool for at least 5 minutes, then skim before stirring in the 2 deseeded chopped tomatoes. Pot into warmed sterilized jars and cover the tops with waxed discs. When completely cold, cover with cellophane or lids, label and store in a cool place.

Cook's tip: If liked, 2 tablespoons of chopped fresh coriander can be added to the finished jelly with the two chopped tomatoes.

MAKES about 1.3 kg/3 lb

900 g/2 lb unblemished firm, ripe tomatoes, rinsed and chopped

1 large orange (preferably unwaxed and organic), unpeeled and scrubbed

2 lemongrass stalks, roughly chopped

5-cm/2-inch piece fresh root ginger, peeled and chopped

1–2 whole star anise

3 whole cloves

900 ml/1 ½ pints water

3 tbsp white wine vinegar

about 900 g/2 lb preserving sugar (see method)

2 tbsp tomato purée

2 firm, ripe tomatoes, deseeded and chopped

41

Traditional chunky marmalade

MAKES about 4.5 kg/10 lb

1.5 kg/3 lb 5 oz Seville oranges, scrubbed

juice from 2 large lemons

3.4 litres/6 pints water

2.7 kg/6 lb preserving sugar

Cut the oranges in half and squeeze out all the juice. Scoop out all the pips from the orange shells and tie up in a small piece of muslin. Slice the peel into small chunks or strips and place in a preserving pan together with the orange and lemon juice and water. Add the bag of pips.

Simmer gently for 1½ hours, or until the peel is very soft and the liquid has reduced by half. Remove the bag of pips, carefully squeezing to remove any juice. Add the sugar and heat, stirring, until the sugar has completely dissolved. Bring to the boil and boil rapidly for about 15 minutes, or until the setting point is reached.

Leave to cool slightly, then pot into warmed sterilized jars and cover the tops with waxed discs. When completely cold, cover with cellophane or lids, label and store in a cool place.

Cook's tip: Seville oranges freeze well, so if you don't have time to make a year's supply of marmalade, buy the oranges when they are in season and freeze for use later in the year.

Ginger citrus marmalade

MAKES about 1.3 kg/3 lb

4 limes (preferably unwaxed and organic), scrubbed

2 large lemons (preferably unwaxed and organic), scrubbed

small piece fresh root ginger, peeled and chopped

1.2 litres/2 pints water

2 tsp ground ginger

about 900 g/2 lb preserving sugar (see method)

115 g/4 oz stem ginger, chopped

Cut off and discard both ends from the limes and lemons and wash thoroughly. Place in a large saucepan together with the chopped root ginger and the water. Bring to the boil then reduce the heat, cover with a tight-fitting lid and simmer for 1½ hours, or until the fruits are very soft.

Cool slightly then drain off the liquid and reserve. Chop the fruits as finely as possible, discarding the pips.

Return the chopped fruits to the rinsed-out saucepan, or use a preserving pan, together with the reserved liquid and the ground ginger. Add the sugar, allowing 450 g/1 lb of sugar for every 600 ml/1 pint of liquid. Heat gently, stirring frequently, until the sugar has completely dissolved. Bring to the boil and boil rapidly for about 15 minutes, or until the setting point is reached.

Leave to cool for 5 minutes then stir in the stem ginger. Pot into warmed sterilized jars and cover the tops with waxed discs. When completely cold, cover with cellophane or lids, label and store in a cool place.

Cook's tip: If the limes and lemons are waxed, scrub vigorously to remove the wax coating.

Lemon and orange marmalade

Before cooking, peel half the fruits very thinly, taking care not to include the bitter white pith, and cut into very fine shreds. Place in a small saucepan, cover with water and simmer for 30 minutes, or until soft. Drain and reserve.

Cut all the fruits into small wedges and place in a large saucepan with any pips and the water. Bring to the boil, then reduce the heat, cover and simmer for about 1½ hours, or until very soft.

Leave to cool slightly, then strain through a jelly bag. Measure the strained juice and return to the pan, or a preserving pan, adding 450 g/1 lb of sugar for every 600 ml/1 pint of liquid. Heat gently, stirring frequently, until the sugar has completely dissolved. Bring to the boil and boil rapidly for 15 minutes, or until the setting point is reached.

Leave to cool slightly then stir in the reserved shredded peel. Pot into warmed sterilized jars and cover the tops with waxed discs. When completely cold, cover with cellophane or lids, label and store in a cool place.

Cook's tip: If liked, the fruit peel can be chopped after simmering in the water, with a very sharp cook's knife or vegetable cleaver.

MAKES about 1.8 kg/4 lb

1.5 kg/3 lb 5 oz lemons and oranges (preferably unwaxed and organic), scrubbed

850 ml/1½ pints water

about 900 g/2 lb preserving sugar (see method)

Reduced sugar marmalade

MAKES about 2.25 kg/5 lb

1.5 kg/3 lb 5 oz oranges
(preferably unwaxed and organic),
washed or scrubbed

450 g/1 lb mandarins (preferably
unwaxed and organic), scrubbed

1.7 litres/3 pints water

1.25 kg/2 lb 12 oz preserving
sugar

Using a vegetable peeler, remove the peel as thinly as possible from 675 g/1 lb 8 oz of the oranges and 225 g/8 oz of the mandarins, then cut the peel into fine shreds. Place in a small saucepan, cover with water and simmer for 30 minutes, or until soft. Drain and reserve.

Peel the remaining oranges and mandarins and cut all the fruits in half, discarding the bitter white pith from them. Reserve the pips and tie up in a piece of muslin together with the rest of the peel. Cut the fruit flesh into chunks and place in a large saucepan together with the water and the bag of pips and peel.

Bring to the boil, then reduce the heat, cover and simmer gently for 1 hour, or until the fruits are very soft. Remove the muslin bag and discard. If preferred, transfer the mixture to a preserving pan. Add the sugar and heat gently, stirring frequently, until the sugar has completely dissolved. Bring to the boil and boil rapidly for 15 minutes, or until the setting point is reached.

Leave to cool for 5–8 minutes then stir in the reserved shredded peel. Pot into warmed sterilized jars and cover the tops with waxed discs. When completely cold, cover with cellophane or lids, label and store in a cool place.

Cook's tip: Other citrus fruits can be used in this recipe, such as grapefruits, limes, clementines and Seville oranges.

Orange and kiwi marmalade

Peel the oranges as thinly as possible and reserve the peel. Cut the fruits in half and squeeze out all the juice. Scoop out the pips and tie the pips up in a small piece of muslin together with the chopped ginger. Finely shred the orange peel and place in a preserving pan. Add the kiwi fruit to the pan together with the water, orange juice and pips.

Bring to the boil, then reduce the heat and simmer gently for 1 hour, or until the peel and fruits are very soft. Remove the pips and discard.

Add the sugar and heat gently, stirring frequently, until the sugar has completely dissolved. Add the butter. Bring to the boil and boil rapidly for about 15 minutes, or until the setting point is reached.

Leave to cool slightly, then pot into warm sterilized jars and cover the tops with waxed discs. When completely cold, cover with cellophane or lids, label and store in a cool place.

Cook's tip: If liked, add a little finely chopped stem ginger to the pan once the setting point is reached and the marmalade has cooled and is ready to pot.

MAKES about 900 g/2 lb

1.5 kg/3 lb 5 oz oranges (preferably unwaxed and organic), washed

5-cm/2-inch piece fresh root ginger, peeled and chopped

6 kiwi fruit, peeled and finely chopped

1.7 litres/3 pints water

1.8 kg/4 lb preserving sugar

1 tsp butter

Apple butter

MAKES about 1 kg/2 lb 4 oz

1.5 kg/3 lb 5 oz Bramley apples, washed

1.2 litres/2 pints sweet cider or apple juice

150 ml/5 fl oz water

150 ml/5 fl oz lemon juice

2 cinnamon sticks, lightly bruised

2 tbsp grated lemon rind

about 450 g/1 lb granulated sugar (see method)

Chop the apples into small chunks, (do not peel or core), discarding any damaged pieces and place in a preserving pan together with the cider or apple juice, water, lemon juice, cinnamon sticks and lemon rind. Bring to the boil, reduce the heat and simmer gently for 30 minutes, stirring occasionally, until the apples have completely collapsed. Remove and discard the cinnamon sticks.

Sieve the mixture then measure the apple pulp and return to the rinsed-out preserving pan. Add the sugar, allow 350 g/12 oz to each 600 ml/1 pint of pulp. Heat gently, stirring constantly, until the sugar has completely dissolved. Continue to cook for a further 15–20 minutes, or until a thick creamy consistency is achieved.

Pot into warmed sterilized jars and cover the tops with waxed discs. When completely cold, cover with lids, label and store in a cool, dark place.

Cook's tips: Store in a cool, dark place for up to 3 months. Once opened, keep in the refrigerator for up to 10 days. If liked, crab apples or windfall apples can be used in place of the cooking apples, and the cinnamon can be replaced with fresh root ginger. If using crab apples, simmer for at least 1 hour, or until soft, then sieve and proceed as in the main recipe.

Plum butter

Place the plums in a preserving pan with the water and bring to the boil. Reduce the heat and simmer gently for 40–50 minutes, or until the plums are very soft and have collapsed. Leave to cool, then sieve and measure the pulp in a measuring jug. Return to the rinsed-out preserving pan.

Add the orange rind and juice with the cinnamon and heat gently for 10 minutes. Stir in the sugar, allowing 350 g/12 oz of sugar to each 600 ml/1 pint of pulp. Heat gently, stirring frequently, until the sugar has completely dissolved. Bring to the boil then boil gently until the mixture has thickened and is creamy.

Pot into warmed sterilized jars and cover the tops with waxed discs. When completely cold, cover with lids, label, store in a cool, dark place and use within 3 months of making. Once opened, store in the refrigerator and use within 2 weeks of opening.

Cook's tip: Add a few sprigs of fresh rosemary or thyme and sage when first cooking the plums, and discard when sieving. This is ideal to serve with both hot and cold meat dishes.

MAKES about 675 g/1 lb 8 oz

1.5 kg/3 lb 5 oz ripe plums, washed and cut in half, stones discarded

600 ml/1 pint water

2 tbsp grated orange rind

300 ml/10 fl oz freshly squeezed orange juice

1½ tsp ground cinnamon

about 900 g/2 lb granulated sugar (see method)

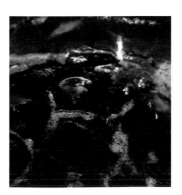

Apple and orange curd

MAKES about 675 g/1 lb 8 oz

450 g/1 lb Bramley apples, peeled, cored and chopped

150 ml/5 fl oz water

2 large oranges (preferably unwaxed and organic), scrubbed

2 eggs, beaten

115 g/4 oz unsalted butter, diced

115 g/4 oz caster sugar

3–4 whole cloves

Place the apples and water in a large saucepan and cook for 10–12 minutes, or until soft and fluffy. Remove from the heat and beat until smooth then sieve. Place the fruit pulp in a heatproof bowl set over a saucepan of gently simmering water.

Finely grate the rind from one of the oranges and squeeze out the juice from both oranges to give 150 ml/5 fl oz juice. Add to the bowl together with the eggs, butter, sugar and cloves. Cook, stirring frequently, until the butter and sugar have melted.

Continue to cook, stirring, until the mixture becomes thick and creamy. Remove the cloves and discard. Pot into warmed sterilized jars and cover the tops with waxed discs. When completely cold, cover with lids, label and store in a cool, dark place.

Cook's tip: Try using other citrus fruits and replace the cloves with cinnamon, star anise or the ripe seeds and juice from 2 passion fruits.

Apricot and passion fruit butter

MAKES about 900 g/2 lb

675 g/1 lb 8 oz fresh ripe apricots, washed and stoned

juice from 2 large oranges to give 150 ml/5 fl oz liquid

600 ml/1 pint water

1 tsp ground allspice

3 ripe passion fruits

175–225 g/6–8 oz granulated sugar, or to taste

Place the apricots in a large saucepan and add the orange juice and water. Bring to the boil, reduce the heat to a simmer, cover with a tight-fitting lid and cook for 45 minutes, or until the apricots have collapsed and are very soft. During cooking, check the liquid has not evaporated. If so, reduce the heat and add a little more water if necessary. Leave to cool slightly then sieve.

Return the sieved apricot pulp to a preserving pan. Add the ground allspice with the seeds and flesh from the passion fruits and 175 g/6 oz sugar. Heat gently, stirring frequently, until the sugar has completely dissolved. Increase the heat slightly and continue to cook, stirring frequently, until thick and creamy. Adjust the sweetness to taste and cook for a little longer if more sugar has been added.

Leave to cool for 5 minutes then spoon into warmed sterilized jars and cover the tops with waxed discs. When completely cold, cover with lids, label and store in a cool, dark place.

Cook's tip: Other fruits can be used in place of the apricots. Try dried mango, pawpaw or dried fruit salad.

Tomato chutney

Place the tomatoes, apples, onions, celery, chilli and sugar in a preserving pan. Tie the coriander seeds in a small piece of muslin then add to the pan together with the water and cook over a gentle heat, stirring occasionally, for 30 minutes, or until the tomatoes and apples have collapsed.

Add both vinegars and the sultanas and bring to the boil, then reduce the heat and simmer for 35–45 minutes, or until a thick consistency is reached.

Leave to cool slightly, discard the coriander seeds then pot into warmed sterilized jars. Cover with non-metallic lids, label and store in a cool place.

Cook's tip: Green tomatoes can also be used for this chutney recipe, if liked. Replace the coriander seeds with fresh root ginger.

MAKES about 3.5 kg/7 lb 10 oz

1.5 kg/3 lb 5 oz firm ripe tomatoes, washed and chopped

450 g/1 lb Bramley apples, peeled, cored and chopped

450 g/1 lb red onions, chopped

1 head of celery, trimmed and chopped, leaves discarded

1 green jalapeño chilli, deseeded and chopped

675 g/1 lb 8 oz demerara sugar

1 tsp coriander seeds, lightly pounded

150 ml/5 fl oz water

600 ml/1 pint malt vinegar

4 tbsp balsamic vinegar

300 g/10$\frac{1}{2}$ oz sultanas

Melon rind pickle

MAKES about 900 g/2 lb

450 g/1 lb melon rind, chopped
into small pieces

2 tbsp salt

600 ml/1 pint very hot water,
plus an extra 850 ml/1½ pints

450 ml/16 fl oz distilled vinegar

450 g/1 lb demerara sugar

3 whole star anise

6 cardamom pods, lightly cracked

2 whole cloves

300 g/10 oz dried apricots,
finely chopped

Place the rind in a non-reactive preserving pan. In a heatproof bowl, dissolve the salt in the 600 ml/1 pint water and pour over the melon rind. Cover and leave to stand for 30 minutes.

Bring the melon rind to the boil and simmer for 30 minutes. Drain and rinse, then return to the pan and cover with the remaining water. Bring to the boil and simmer for 10 minutes. Drain, cover with fresh water, bring to the boil and boil again for 10 minutes. Remove from the heat and leave overnight.

The next day, drain the melon rind and return to the non-reactive preserving pan. Add the sugar, together with the spices, tied up in a small piece of muslin, and the apricots.

Simmer over a gentle heat for 1 hour, or until the melon rind is clear. Remove the spices and pot into warmed sterilized jars. Cover with non-metallic lids, label and store in a cool place.

Cook's tip: If liked, a little green food colouring can be added at the end of cooking.

Sweet mango preserve

MAKES about 1.5 kg/3 lb 5 oz

4 ripe mangos, about 900 g/2 lb, peeled and finely chopped

1–2 red chillies, deseeded and chopped

5-cm/2-inch piece fresh root ginger, peeled and grated

grated rind and juice of 2 lemons (preferably unwaxed and organic), scrubbed

600 ml/1 pint water

450 g/1 lb light muscovado sugar

175 g/6 oz golden sultanas

2–3 tbsp balsamic vinegar

Place the mangos, chillies and ginger in a preserving pan. Add the lemon rind and juice and stir in the water. Bring to the boil and simmer for 20 minutes.

Add the sugar and heat gently until the sugar has completely dissolved. Bring to the boil and boil for 10 minutes, or until a thick consistency is reached. Stir in the sultanas and balsamic vinegar and cook for a further 5 minutes.

Leave to cool slightly. Pot into warmed sterilized jars and cover the tops with waxed discs. When completely cold, cover with cellophane or lids, label and store in a cool place.

Cook's tip: Other flavours can be used instead of the chillies and ginger, if liked. Try adding 2 vanilla pods, or 4 star anise, 6 lightly cracked cardamom pods and 2 whole cloves, tied in a small piece of muslin. Remove from the preserve before potting.

Sweet beetroot preserve

MAKES about 2.25 kg/5 lb

900 g/2 lb raw beetroot, peeled and grated or finely chopped

225 g/8 oz onions, finely chopped

450 g/1 lb Bramley apples, peeled, cored and finely chopped

grated rind and juice of 2 large oranges, scrubbed

850 ml/1½ pints malt vinegar

300 ml/10 fl oz water

450 g/1 lb demerara sugar

225 g/8 oz seedless raisins

Place the beetroot in a preserving pan with the onions, apples, orange rind and juice. Add the vinegar and water and bring to the boil. Reduce the heat and simmer for 15 minutes.

Add the sugar and heat gently, stirring frequently, until the sugar has completely dissolved, then stir in the raisins. Simmer for a further 30 minutes, or until the beetroot is soft.

Leave to cool slightly. Pot into warmed sterilized jars and cover the tops with waxed discs. When completely cold, cover with cellophane or lids, label and store in a cool place.

Cook's tip: If preferred, replace the raisins with an equal quantity of canned cherries or chopped maraschino cherries.

Berry preserve

Place all the fruits in a large preserving pan with the lemon juice and sugar. Heat gently, stirring occasionally, until the sugar has completely dissolved. Add the butter.

Bring to the boil and boil rapidly for 3 minutes, then remove from the heat and stir in the pectin. Leave to cool before skimming. Pot into warmed sterilized jars and cover the tops with waxed discs. When completely cold, cover with cellophane or lids, label and store in a cool place.

Cook's tip: Make sure that the fruits are undamaged and free from blemishes.

MAKES about 1.8 kg/4 lb

900 g/2 lb assorted berries, such as blueberries, cranberries, raspberries and strawberries, hulled and rinsed

3 tbsp lemon juice

900 g/2 lb granulated sugar

1 tsp butter

225 ml/8 fl oz liquid pectin

Raspberry and apple preserve

MAKES about 900 g/2 lb

600 g/1 lb 5 oz Bramley cooking apples, peeled, cored and chopped

600 g/1 lb 5 oz fresh ripe raspberries, rinsed

225 ml/8 fl oz lemon juice

450 g/1 lb granulated sugar

225 ml/8 fl oz liquid pectin

Layer all the fruits with the lemon juice, sugar and pectin in a large clean mixing bowl. Cover tightly and leave overnight.

The next day, stir well and pour the mixture into a preserving pan. Bring to the boil, stirring occasionally, and boil for 4 minutes. Remove from the heat and leave to cool for 5 minutes.

Pot into warmed sterilized jars and cover the tops with waxed discs. When completely cold, cover with cellophane or lids, label and store in a cool place. Once opened, store in the refrigerator and use within 10 days.

Cook's tips: Other berries can be used in place of the raspberries. Try blackberries with orange in place of the lemon juice.

Pepper pot preserve

MAKES about 1.3 kg/3 lb

450 g/1 lb Bramley apples, peeled, cored and chopped

450 g/1 lb onions, thinly sliced

3–4 garlic cloves, sliced

2–4 serrano chillies, deseeded and finely sliced

900 g/2 lb assorted coloured peppers, deseeded and finely chopped

450 g/1 lb demerara sugar, or add a little extra if a sweeter relish is preferred

1–3 tsp Tabasco sauce, or to taste

300 ml/10 fl oz red wine vinegar

85 ml/3 fl oz balsamic vinegar

Place the apples in a preserving pan together with the onions, garlic, chillies and peppers. Sprinkle with the sugar then add the Tabasco sauce. Simmer over a gentle heat for 15 minutes, stirring frequently, until the apples and onions are beginning to soften.

Add the vinegars and continue to simmer for 40 minutes, or until a thick consistency is reached and the liquid is absorbed. Check the sweetness and if necessary add a little extra sugar, then simmer for a further 10 minutes.

Remove from the heat and leave to cool for 5 minutes. Pot into warmed sterilized jars and cover the tops with waxed discs. When completely cold, cover with cellophane or lids, label and store in a cool place.

Cook's tip: If a more fiery relish is preferred, use hotter chillies such as bird's eye chilli or habañero.

index